Stefan Höppel

High Frequency Trading

Economic Necessity or Threat to the Economy?

Anchor Compact

Höppel, Stefan: High Frequency Trading: Economic Necessity or Threat to the Economy? Hamburg, Anchor Academic Publishing 2014

Buch-ISBN: 978-3-95489-219-8
PDF-eBook-ISBN: 978-3-95489-719-3
Druck/Herstellung: Anchor Academic Publishing, Hamburg, 2014

Bibliografische Information der Deutschen Nationalbibliothek:
Die Deutsche Nationalbibliothek verzeichnet diese Publikation in der Deutschen Nationalbibliografie; detaillierte bibliografische Daten sind im Internet über http://dnb.d-nb.de abrufbar

Bibliographical Information of the German National Library:
The German National Library lists this publication in the German National Bibliography. Detailed bibliographic data can be found at: http://dnb.d-nb.de

All rights reserved. This publication may not be reproduced, stored in a retrieval system or transmitted, in any form or by any means, electronic, mechanical, photocopying, recording or otherwise, without the prior permission of the publishers.

Das Werk einschließlich aller seiner Teile ist urheberrechtlich geschützt. Jede Verwertung außerhalb der Grenzen des Urheberrechtsgesetzes ist ohne Zustimmung des Verlages unzulässig und strafbar. Dies gilt insbesondere für Vervielfältigungen, Übersetzungen, Mikroverfilmungen und die Einspeicherung und Bearbeitung in elektronischen Systemen.

Die Wiedergabe von Gebrauchsnamen, Handelsnamen, Warenbezeichnungen usw. in diesem Werk berechtigt auch ohne besondere Kennzeichnung nicht zu der Annahme, dass solche Namen im Sinne der Warenzeichen- und Markenschutz-Gesetzgebung als frei zu betrachten wären und daher von jedermann benutzt werden dürften.

Die Informationen in diesem Werk wurden mit Sorgfalt erarbeitet. Dennoch können Fehler nicht vollständig ausgeschlossen werden und die Diplomica Verlag GmbH, die Autoren oder Übersetzer übernehmen keine juristische Verantwortung oder irgendeine Haftung für evtl. verbliebene fehlerhafte Angaben und deren Folgen.

Alle Rechte vorbehalten

© Anchor Academic Publishing, ein Imprint der Diplomica® Verlag GmbH
http://www.diplom.de, Hamburg 2014
Printed in Germany

Table of Contents

List of abbreviations III

1 Introduction 1

   1.1 Problem 1

   1.2 Aim 1

   1.3 Research Questions 2

   1.4 Scientific Method 2

   1.5 Structure of the paper... 2

2 Fundamentals of HFT 3

   2.1 History of HFT and its presence in current markets 3

      2.1.1 Algorithmic Trading (AT) 3

      2.1.2 Definition and characteristics of HFT 3

      2.1.3 HFT's fraction of market activity in the US and Europe 4

   2.2. Technology used for HFT 5

      2.2.1 Software for HFT 5

      2.2.2 Hardware for HFT 5

   2.3 Users of HFT 6

   2.4 Strategies of HFTs 7

      2.4.1 Liquidity Provision (Market Making) 7

      2.4.2 Liquidity Detection 8

      2.4.3 Arbitrage 9

         2.4.3.1 Market Neutral Arbitrage ("Pairs Trading").............................. 9

         2.4.3.2 Cross Asset-, Cross Market- & ETF-Arbitrage 9

3 The effect of HFT on capital markets and

the Economic Neoclassical Theory 10

   3.1 The Economic Neoclassical Theory and its relation to HFT 10

   3.2 The effect of HFT on liquidity... 11

   3.3 The effect of HFT on price discovery... 14

   3.4 The effect of HFT on volatility.. 16

4 The regulation and supervision of HFT 19

    4.1 Manipulation and the importance of regulation and supervision of HFT 19

    4.2 The Flash Crash 20

    4.3 General regulatory measures 21

        4.3.1 Unfiltered/Naked Sponsored Access 21

        4.3.2 Flash Orders 22

    4.4 The regulatory response to the Flash Crash 22

        4.4.1 Circuit breakers 22

        4.4.2 Stub quotes and erroneous trades 23

    4.5 Other possible regulatory measures and their effect on volatility 24

        4.5.1 Tobin tax 24

        4.5.2 Short sale constraints 24

5 Conclusion 26

References 29

Table of figures 36

List of abbreviations

AT	Algorithmic Trading/Algorithmic Trader
ATs	Algorithmic Traders
ATP	Algorithmic Trading Program
CFTC	Commodity Futures Trading Commission
CME	Chicago Mercantile Exchange
CRSP	Center for Research in Security Prices
DJIA	Dow Jones Industrial Average
ETF	Exchange Traded Fund
ETS	Electronic Trading System
Eurex	Eurex Exchange – European Exchange AG
FINRA	Financial Industry Regulatory Authority
HFT	High Frequency Trading/High Frequency Trader
HFTs	High Frequency Traders
ICE	Intercontinental Exchange, Incorporated
ITS	Intermarket Trading System
NASD	National Association of Securities Dealers
NASDAQ	National Association of Securities Dealers Automated Quotations
NBBO	National Best Bid and Offer
NMS	National Market System
NYSE	New York Stock Exchange
SEC	Securities and Exchange Commission
UK	United Kingdom
US (=USA)	United States of America
USD	United States Dollar(s)
WAN	Wide Area Network

1 Introduction

1.1 Problem

In the last four decades, technological progress led to an electrification of stock trading systems. Traders were enabled to place their orders, which were later processed via electronic networks, with the help of computers. Soon they realized that the profitability of trading strategies could be increased by employing computer algorithms to trade autonomously, reducing time needed to analyze information, publish quotes as well as trigger and process trades. This led to the implementation of Algorithmic Trading (AT). High Frequency Trading (HFT) is a subset of AT, at which financial instruments are traded by algorithms at very high speed.

The past has shown that negative developments on capital markets are intensified by HFT. Andrei Kirilenko explains in his work "The Flash Crash: The Impact of High Frequency Trading on an Electronic Market" that HFT did not trigger the Flash Crash but intensified the volatility that resulted from the event. Also on the 19th of October 1987, "Black Monday", the increasing computerization of stock trading processes led to a significant price drop. As a consequence, the high and still growing market share of HFT leads to an increase in risk that a simple correction turns into a serious drop in prices causing market instability. Theoretically HFT should increase efficiency in financial markets. However, due to the empirical observation mentioned above, it seems that HFT takes effect the other way round. It seems that, at least under certain circumstances, HFT enlarges volatility. This cannot be explained by the economic neoclassical theory. This problem is discussed in a lot of literature in which several different approaches have been made to explain it.

1.2 Aim

The aim of this paper is to discuss why HFT cannot be fully explained by the neoclassical theory of economics. Therefore, the controversial positions in literature will be presented and discussed. Primarily, its negative influence on volatility seems to contravene the modern finance. Furthermore, in the course of this work it will be illustrated that, by employing strict regulation of financial markets, this negative impact cannot be reduced to a sufficient extent in order for HFT to be characterized as market optimizing, according to the neoclassical theory of economics.

1.3 Research Questions

As a result of this objective, the following research questions arise:

1) Is there research that perfectly describes the effect of HFT on capital markets or is it, based on a comparison of different researchers' findings, necessary to combine these findings in order to ensure a realistic description of the matter?
2) Can the negative effect of HFT on market quality be reduced, by employing strict regulation of financial markets, to a sufficient extent in order for HFT to be explained by the neoclassical theory of economics?

1.4 Scientific Method

The scientific method is comprised of literature research. For this paper mainly working papers and professional articles have been used as references.

1.5 Structure of the paper

In the first part of this study, the basics of HFT are explained, with reference to its history, the presence of HFT in current markets as well as its users and their strategies.

The following chapter deals with the effect of HFT on capital markets and its capability of optimizing financial markets according to the neoclassical theory of economics. Findings on the effect of HFT on liquidity, price discovery and volatility in financial markets are examined.

The importance of regulation and supervision of HFT as well as regulatory measures and their influence on market quality are topics of the third section of this paper. Also, the "Flash Crash of May 06, 2010", an incident impelling the regulation of HFT, is illustrated in detail.

A conclusion is shown in the last part of the paper.

2 Fundamentals of HFT

2.1 History of HFT and its presence in current markets

Within the last 40 years, a drastic change in trading processes of securities and other financial products has taken place. Technological development has led to an electrification of trading systems, which extensively replaced physical trading floors *(see Gomber et al. 2011, p. 8)*. Lee defines ETSs as exchange-systems for financial instruments, in which buyers and sellers are brought together *(see Lee 1998, p. 282)*. The first computer-assisted trading system – today it is known as NASDAQ – was put into operation by the NASD in the USA, in 1971. Since then, market participants have continuously aimed to improve trading processes *(see Gomber et al. 2011, p. 8)*. Today almost all markets are electronic. According to Jain, the leading exchanges in 101 of 120 sample countries have electronic trading, 85 of them act fully electronically, without floor trading *(see Jain 2005, p. 2965)*.

2.1.1 Algorithmic Trading (AT)

Electronic trading systems execute their trades with the help of computer algorithms. These use direct market access in order to autonomously make investment decisions, based on observed and analyzed real-time market information, submit orders and manage them after submission without human intervention of any kind. AT can be defined as the use of such means for trading *(see Hendershott/Jones/Menkveld 2011, p. 1; see Gomber et al. 2011, p. 14)*.

The algorithms can be programmed in various ways, depending on the trading strategies the market participants aim to execute with the help of AT. Algorithms for AT are generally characterized by holding periods of up to several weeks and months as well as the aim to achieve a particular benchmark, among other things. Some strategies, however, may require algorithms that have different features for their execution. Such might be applicable to HFT, a subgroup of AT *(see Gomber et al. 2011, p. 14)*.

2.1.2 Definition and characteristics of HFT

As with AT, there is not only one correct definition of HFT. Basically, algorithms used by HFTs and those necessary for general AT, have common characteristics. Both are used by professional traders to observe market data and initiate and manage trades by using direct market access *(see Gomber et al. 2011, p. 15)*. However, there are certain differences. Unlike ATs, HFTs usually do several thousands of trades per day *(see Hasbrouck/Saar 2010, p. 1)* on their own accounts *(see Hasbrouck/Saar 2010, p. 13)*. The holding periods of financial instruments traded that way amount to several milliseconds *(see Authority for the Financial Markets 2010, p. 8)*. Algorithms that execute HFT-strategies generally update, cancel and delete their orders frequently, for the purpose of extracting small profits per trade. Within the last four years, the ratio of orders to completed trades has changed from 20:1 to more than 50:1 *(see Watson 2011, p. 59)*. Focusing on highly liquid financial instruments helps to achieve a flat position at the end of the day, meaning that holding positions overnight is avoided *(see Gomber et al. 2011, p. 15)*.

2.1.3 HFT's fraction of market activity in the US and Europe

The market shares of AT and HFT are difficult to measure, as both human traders and trading computers submit their orders electronically. Most algorithms send their orders electronically to an exchange, which is why the rate of electronic message traffic is commonly used as a proxy for the amount of AT – this is also applicable to HFT – on the market *(see Hendershott/Jones/Menkveld 2011, p. 6)*. *Figure 1* illustrates the best estimates from several institutions of the market share of HFT.

Origin	Date of publication	US	Europe	Australia
TABB Group	Sep-09	61%		
Celent	Dec-09	42% of US trade volume	Rapidly growing	
Rosenblatt Securities	Sep-09	66%	~35% and growing fast	
Broogard	Nov-10	68% of Nasdaq trade volume		
Jarnecic and Snape	Jun-10		20% and 32% of LSE total trades and 19% and 28% of total volume	
Tradeworx	Apr-10	40%		
ASX	Feb-10			10% of ASX trade volume
Swinburne	Nov-10	70%	40%	
TABB Group	Jan-11		35% of overall UK market and 77% of turnover in continuous markets	

Figure 1: HFT Market shares from industry and academic studies *(Gomber et al. 2011, p. 73)*.

The results show a growing market share of HFT over the last five years. An estimate of WM Gruppe, Börse-Zeitung, which is not illustrated in *Figure 1*, indicates that, in

2011, HFT-activity amounted to 70% of the volume traded in securities in the US. In the same year, 40% of the stock trades of Deutsche Börse AG were executed by HFTs, and the trend is still growing. Eurex, one of the world's leading derivatives exchanges, is expecting a growth rate of 20% per year in the field of automated trading, due to expected increases in the efficiency of arbitrage-trading, faster market-making, rationalization and further automation of trading, among other things *(see Gomber 2011, p. 19)*.

2.2. Technology used for HFT

HFTs need a comprehensive IT-infrastructure in order to be able to execute their trades within milliseconds or microseconds. The lower the time needed to receive market information, make investment decisions and place an order at an exchange, the more profitable is the system for its user. This is why HFTs strive to minimize this so called latency period *(see Hasbrouck/Saar 2010, p. 1)*. HFTs try to get the advantage over other traders by employing high performance supercomputers and obtaining information faster than others, for instance through direct connections of their servers to exchanges *(see Angel/Harris/Spatt 2010, p. 38)*. They continuously aim to optimize their processes in terms of software as well as hardware.

2.2.1 Software for HFT

Depending on their strategies (see chapter "2.4 Strategies of HF-Traders"), HFTs use different software, including standard trading programs available on the market as well as individually programmed and customized software. Every piece of software consists of a front-end, the user interface that shows the information the HFT needs, and a back-end, the actual algorithm. Such algorithms are the core of the software and a prerequisite for successful HFT, as they obtain and analyze market information and make investment decisions based on these data. The fewer and simpler the required information is, the faster this process can be executed *(see Gomolka 2011, p. 198)*. This results in lower latency and higher profitability of the system.

2.2.2 Hardware for HFT

Besides software, the quality of hardware has a big influence on an HFT's success. Modern technology makes it possible for electronic signals to travel at the speed of light *(see Kumar et al. 2011, p. 4)*. According to Yan Ohayon, this fastest possible way of transmitting electric signals actually slows the orders of HFTs down, due to HFTs' enormous capacity in terms of speed which is created by the software *(see*

Watson 2011, p. 56). For the fastest possible data processing and execution of their international trading activity, HFTs need a WAN, a network connecting multiple servers *(see Zadorozhny/Raschid/Gal 2008, p. 1)*. These servers are located as close as possible to the servers of the exchanges the HFT operates on ("co-location"), transferring the information that is generated by the exchanges' servers to a control center that is ideally located half way between the respective trading venues. As such "co-locations" are very valuable to HFTs, exchanges rent them to the traders *(Sietmann 2011, p. 152)*.

Figure 2 illustrates the development of execution times of small market orders for stocks listed on NYSE and NASDAQ (in seconds), from 2001 to 2009. It is recognizable that further automation of trading processes leads to an increase in execution speed *(see Angel/Harris/Spatt 2010, p. 22)*. Today, according to Kumar et al. (2011), execution times of one millisecond and less are available at numerous American trading venues *(see Kumar et al. 2011, p. 4)*.

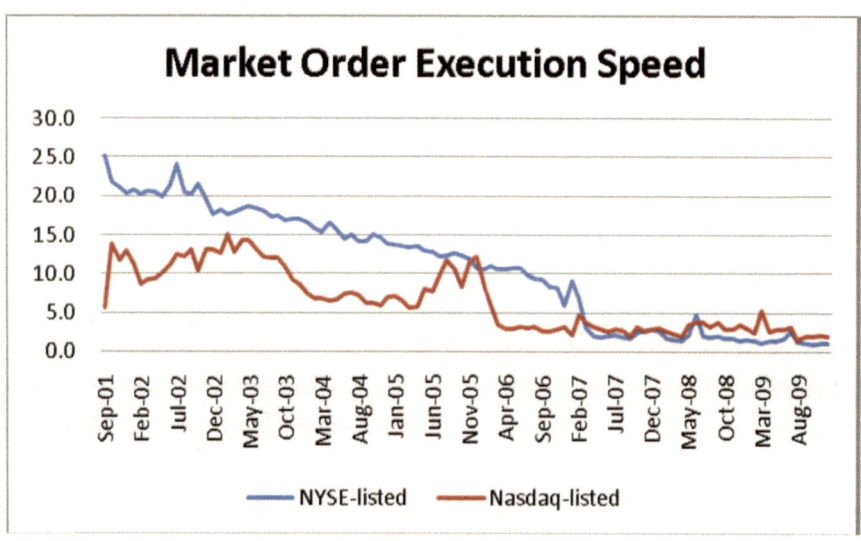

Figure 2: Market Order Execution Speed. Rule 605 data from Thomson for all eligible market orders (100-9999 shares) *(see Angel/Harris/Spatt 2010, p. 22)*.

2.3 Users of HFT

AT can be separated into two branches with different characteristics: (1) Agency trading: The automated execution of trades in the course of which a trader invests his clients' capital. The purpose of such deals is to profit from an investment rather than trading itself. (2) Proprietary trading: A method of using strategies for the purpose of pattern detection in order to generate profits from trading itself *(see Hasbrouck/Saar 2010, p. 12)*.

As illustrated in chapter "2.1.2 Definition and characteristics of HFT", HFT is characterized by the investment of the trader's own capital. As a consequence, agency traders, such as investment banks, can only employ HFT to maximize the profits they earn from their core business, the service they get paid for by their clients. Proprietary trading firms, however, are meant to generate profits from the trading of financial instruments, using their own capital *(see Hasbrouck/Saar 2010, p. 12)*. These companies represent a fraction of approximately 2% of the 20.000 hedge funds, mutual funds and brokers operating in US-equities. Businesses like RGM usually do not employ more than 120 scientists and software engineers for the development of technology that automatically monitors market information and trades based on these observed data. Doing that, without taking into account the real value of a company, currency or commodity, this economic sector generates an annual profit of several billion USD – USD 7.2 billion during the economic and financial crisis, in 2009 *(see Foroohar 2010)*. The most important of the strategies HFTs pursue, when trading based on monitored and examined market data, are explained in chapter "2.4 Strategies of HFTs" of this paper.

2.4 Strategies of HFTs

HFT itself is not a strategy. The strategies used by HFTs are often traditional and well known to the market. What makes them so efficient is the use of modern technology to employ them. Depending on their business models, HFTs have various different strategies *(see Gomber et al. 2011, p. 24)*. In the course of this chapter, three well known and frequently used strategies are introduced: Liquidity Provision (Market Making), Liquidity Detection and Arbitrage.

2.4.1 Liquidity Provision (Market Making)

By submitting buy- and sell-limit orders at the same time, HFTs provide liquidity to market participants who want to trade. This way they create "artificial liquidity", liquidity that results from contractual obligations instead of trading interest *(see Gomber/Lutat 2007, p. 11)*. Such market makers usually profit from (1) buying at the bid price and selling at the ask price and (2) receiving liquidity rebates from trading venues *(see Gomber et al. 2011, p. 24)*.

Buying at a certain price and selling at a higher price, as described in (1), is an HFT-strategy called "spread capturing". If this principle is followed in the majority of trades executed by HFTs, it can contribute significantly to the revenues of these firms *(see Gomber et al. 2011, p. 26)*. (2) Outlines a strategy, employed by HFTs, that allows them to generate revenues from trading fee discounts and liquidity rebates they receive from exchanges. Many trading venues charge lower fees and offer incentives to liquidity providers while making trading more expensive for liquidity demanders *(see Gomber/Lutat 2007, pp. 10-12)*. They do that in order to attract more of such passive traders (liquidity providers), and further to make it affordable to submit more limit orders to always reflect the total market information. Thus they narrow the bid-ask-spread *(see Gomber et al. 2011, p. 26)* and improve market quality. HFTs can, but are not obliged to, pursue a market-making-strategy. However, such strategies are frequently adopted by HFTs *(see Gomber et al. 2011, p. 17)*, as they can be related to certain benefits, such as maker fees *(see Authority for the Financial Markets 2010, p. 15)*.

2.4.2 Liquidity Detection

HFTs employing liquidity detection strategies use ultra-high speed technology in order to analyze the market activity of other traders for the purpose of profiting from information they have *(see Gomber et al. 2011, p. 28)*. HFTs "sniff out" the market in order to find out if a large order is placed. That would be an indicator that a market participant has valuable information based on which he wants to trade. This can be detected by simply posting an immediate-or-cancel order, priced at the bid-ask-midpoint, in the market. If the order is executed, this might indicate that a large order is posted *(see Reynolds 2011, p. 24)*. The ability of trading much faster than other market participants based on this data, gives HFTs an enormous advantage *(see Gomber et al. 2011, p. 28)*. For this reason, such strategies can be profitable for HFTs, but they often are a matter of concern for institutional investors and other non-HFTs. Jones (2013) describes this problem with the help of an example: If an institutional investor is buying shares, HFTs might be able to deduce that from information detected on the market. As a consequence, they can drive the price of these shares up and sell them at a higher price, probably even to the institutional investor who initially posted the buy-order *(see Jones 2013, p. 9)*. This means that the profit of HFTs employing such strategies can be a loss for other investors. According to Brogaard (2010), HFTs as a whole do not engage in such "anticipatory trading", but he also states that, due to the complexity and large variety of HFT-strategies as well as their influence on his approach to detect anticipatory trading, it cannot be concluded that there is no anticipatory trading *(Brogaard 2010, p. 22)*.

2.4.3 Arbitrage

Arbitrage opportunities are market conditions in which market participants can generate profit, almost without taking any kind of risk. The usage of ultra-high speed technology makes it possible for HFTs to take such chances, as they often only last for split seconds. Theoretically, the arbitrage strategies outlined in this chapter can also be employed by non-HFTs, but due to the speed advantage of HFTs it is very likely that they will get their trades filled first *(see Gomber et al. 2011, p. 26)*.

2.4.3.1 Market Neutral Arbitrage ("Pairs Trading")

Companies employing a market neutral arbitrage strategy are interested in financial instruments whose prices have historically correlated. They take advantage of situations, in which a spread between the two prices occurs. This means that, when the spread is widening, they buy the relatively cheaper instrument while shorting the higher priced. They expect the two prices to converge again and thus make a profit by then liquidating the two positions *(see Mori/Ziobrowski 2011, p. 409)*.

2.4.3.2 Cross Asset-, Cross Market- & ETF-Arbitrage

According to the law of one price, two identical financial instruments that trade simultaneously in different markets – free of tariffs, transportation costs and other costs related to trading – must trade for the same price in all these markets *(Chami Batista/Borges da Silveira 2008, p. 3)*. Employers of cross market-arbitrage strategies take advantage of pricing inefficiencies across markets. Profits are generated by buying the financial instrument at the relatively cheaper price on one market and selling it at the higher price on the other market, but only if the spread between the two prices is higher than the total transaction fees *(see Gomber et al. 2011, p. 28)*.

Cross asset-arbitrage follows a similar principle. Gomber et al. (2011) explain it with the help of an example: If an option is overpriced relative to its asset, shorting the option in combination with a long position in the underlying can be a promising strategy. The same method can be used in order to profit from inefficiencies between the prices of an ETF and its underlying *(see Gomber et al. 2011, p. 28)*.

3 The effect of HFT on capital markets and the Economic Neoclassical Theory

3.1 The Economic Neoclassical Theory and its relation to HFT

"The neoclassical theory of economics" is a broad term, used to explain the findings of several schools of economic thought. The numerous approaches to neoclassical economics make it difficult to clearly define the term *(see Dequech 2007, p. 280)*. However, the economic neoclassical theory embodies their approaches to price discovery, income, employment levels, inflation rates as well as supply and demand, assuming that (1) agents act individually, (2) in order to maximize their profits or their personal well-being, (3) alleging rational behavior *(see Brennan/Moehler 2010, pp. 946-947)*. Brennan and Moehler (2010) illustrate that neoclassical economics describes the determination of prices based on the subjective preferences of a buyer and a seller, rather than objective matters only *(see Brennan/Moehler 2010, p. 946)*. Since the 1970s, the neoclassical economic theory has been taught at universities and used to describe the economic system and its functionality. However, several financial crises and bubbles proved incorrect the claim that deregulation of financial markets, which the theory stands for, automatically brings stability. Nevertheless, the system's victory over central command economies was seen as a proof of its validity. The financial crisis of 2007-2009, however, showed that this theory cannot be solely used for policy making or to fully explain economic systems, as markets are not efficient and self-regulating. According to neoclassical economics – for the purpose of maintaining financial and price stability, fast growth and fair income distribution – the protection of property rights and contracts as well as the balancing of public finances suffices. This proved to be wrong during the financial crisis of 2007-2009. As a consequence, a certain critique of neoclassical economics is justified and even necessary for the implementation of theories that describe our economic system in a better way, being of historical-deductive rather than hypothetical-deductive nature. There are several theories that – in combination with neoclassical economics – might be adequate to illustrate how our system works *(see Bresser-Pereira 2012, pp. 3-6)*. Nevertheless, parts of the neoclassical theory of economics are still crucial for the correct explanation of economic systems, including supply, demand, prices and growth, which are important topics in financial markets. According to Brennan and Moehler (2010), neoclassical economics still dominates today's economic system *(see Brennan/Moehler 2010, p. 946)*.

In this paper, efficient and self-regulating markets are also understood as optimized markets in the sense of the neoclassical theory of economics. The self-regulating market is defined by Polanyi as an economy, which is directed by nothing but market prices, organizing the entire economic life without external interference *(see Polanyi 1944, p. 43)*. Fama proved validity of the statement, that in efficient markets all relevant information is "fully reflected" in prices *(see Fama 1970, pp. 384 and 416)*. The price level at which all information is reflected in the prices is often referred to as "equilibrium" or "efficient prices". Grossman and Stiglitz (1980) explain in their work that if equilibrium is defined as a price level at which all arbitrage opportunities are eliminated, markets cannot be efficient, as prices will naturally fluctuate in competitive markets *(Grossman/Stiglitz 1980, p. 393)*. The logical consequence of this statement is that HFT proves the inefficiency of markets by taking advantage of arbitrage opportunities, but at the same time contributes to market efficiency, as it helps to diminish arbitrage opportunities and equilibrate market prices.

Overall, a system like HFT is understood to contribute to market optimization in the sense of the neoclassical theory of economics and thus to be fully explained by this theory, if it is consistent with the assumptions of the neoclassical theory of economics that are explained in the first paragraph of this chapter. Furthermore, HFT may not threaten market quality, even if the market is not regulated. It is also necessary that the system supports the reflection of the total information in market prices and it may not have any characteristics that could cause an increase in the deviation from this equilibrium price. This is the fundamental thought, based on which this paper examines the real impact of HFT on capital markets as well as the adequacy of the neoclassical theory of economics to explain HFT. In the following, the impact of HFT on capital markets is analyzed, referring to its effect on liquidity (see chapter "3.2 The effect of HFT on liquidity"), price discovery (see chapter "3.3 The effect of HFT on price discovery") and volatility (see chapter "3.4 The effect of HFT on volatility").

3.2 The effect of HFT on liquidity

A market can be described as liquid, when trader can buy or sell an asset without causing a substantial change in its price. Large buy-side institutional investors often blame HFT for the fugacity of liquidity in today's financial markets. According to them, the large number of orders submitted by HFTs and their high cancellation rate, as explained in chapter "2.1.2 Definition and characteristics of HFT", make it very difficult for non-HFTs to access liquidity *(Foresight et al. 2012, pp. 46-47)*. The literature on the matter, however, also stresses the positive aspects of HFT, concerning liquidity. In this chapter the overall impact of HFT on liquidity and, as a consequence on financial markets, is described comparing various expert findings.

Hendershott, Jones and Menkveld (2011) explain the effects of AT – as a subcategory of AT, the results are also applicable to HFT – on liquidity by analyzing the impact of the implementation of the auto-quote system at NYSE on the matter *(see Hendershott/Jones/Menkveld 2011, p. 1)*. Spreads are used as liquidity measures. Defining effective spreads as the difference between the midpoint of the bid and ask quotes and the actual transaction price, they explain that a higher effective spread means lower liquidity of the stock. *(see Hendershott/Jones/Menkveld 2011, pp. 7-10)*. The results of their research suggest that, especially for large stocks, the automation of stock trading processes narrows spreads, revealing that AT improves liquidity *(see Hendershott/Jones/Menkveld 2011, p. 10)* which contributes to market quality.

Brogaard (2010) examines the effect of HFT on liquidity, referring to inside-quotes, the prices at which orders are executed, and the depth of liquidity provided by HFTs, meaning the volume of a financial product that is traded by HFTs. He performs several analyses in order to determine HFTs' book depth as well as the factors that have an impact on the fraction of time in which HFTs provide the best bid and offer *(see Brogaard 2010, p. 33)*. The results suggest that HFTs supply more liquidity in stocks of companies with high market capitalization than in small stocks, but generally they provide liquidity of lower depth than non-HFTs. Overall his findings indicate that HFT tends to improve market quality *(see Brogaard 2010, p. 40)*.

Hendershott and Riordan (2009) study under which market conditions ATs supply and demand liquidity. Their analyses show that ATs "sniff out" the market for information and liquidity, as explained in chapter "2.4.2 Liquidity Detection" of this paper. They supply liquidity on approximately 50% of the volume traded *(see Hendershott/Riordan 2009, p. 18)*, especially under market conditions when it is scarce and thus expensive *(see Hendershott/Riordan 2009, p. 20)*. ATs are more likely to demand liquidity when there is plenty in the market *(see Hendershott/Riordan 2009, p. 13)*, especially when it is mainly supplied by humans *(see Hendershott/Riordan 2009, p. 14)*. They also increase their liquidity demand when spreads are narrow and thus they get liquidity at a low price *(see Hendershott/Riordan 2009, p. 13)*. Hendershott and Riordan conclude that the ATP, which was approved by the German competition authority, improved liquidity *(see Hendershott/Riordan 2009, p. 23)*.

Hasbrouck and Saar (2010) examine the impact of low latency trading on liquidity by analyzing 10-minute trading periods at NASDAQ in 2007 and 2008, using three measures of liquidity: (1) the average effective spread of all trades observed in the relevant time interval, meaning the absolute difference between the transaction price and the midquote, (2) the spread, computed by deducting the bid price from the ask price, and (3) the near depth, the weighted average number of shares that deviate less than 10 cent from the best offer *(see Hasbrouck/Saar 2010, p. 22)*. Their results suggest that low latency trading narrows spreads and increases depth in the limit order book *(see Hasbrouck/Saar 2010, p. 25)*, indicating that this form of trading increases liquidity and contributes to market quality.

Menkveld (2013) describes the impact of the presence of HFT on Dutch index stocks for a period from 2007 to 2008. He defines trades that are executed immediately as aggressive and liquidity demanding, whereas those that are added to the limit order book and not executed immediately are referred to as passive and liquidity supplying *(see Menkveld 2013, p. 8)*. His research results indicate that approximately 78% of HF-trades are passive (liquidity supplying) *(see Menkveld 2013, p. 22)*. The entry of HFT into Chi-X (a European equities exchange) caused a 50% drop in the bid-ask spread *(see Menkveld 2013, p. 3)*. The large number of passive trades as well as the reduction of the spread, indicate that HFT contributes to liquidity and thus improves market quality.

The researchers, who examine the impact of HFT on liquidity, mainly focus on the narrowness of spreads and the supply and demand of liquidity. Hendershott, Jones and Menkveld (2013) as well as Hasbrouck and Saar (2010) find that low-latency trading narrows spreads, which increases overall market quality *((see Hendershott/Jones/Menkveld 2011, pp. 7-10); (see Hasbrouck/Saar 2010, p. 25))*. According to Hendershott and Riordan (2009), HFTs provide liquidity on roughly 50% of the volume traded *(see Hendershott/Riordan 2009, p. 18)*. Menkveld (2013) illustrates that they supply liquidity with approximately 78% of their trades *(see Menkveld 2013, p. 22)*. Brogaard (2010), however, finds that HFTs provide liquidity of lower depth than non-HFTs *(see Brogaard 2010, p. 40)*. Furthermore, Hendershott and Riordan (2009) describe that HFTs supply liquidity when it is expensive and demand it when it is cheap *(see Hendershott/Riordan 2009, pp. 20 and 13)*, indicating that non-HFTs could either demand liquidity when it is plentiful or pay a high price for it.

3.3 The effect of HFT on price discovery

Brogaard, Hendershott and Riordan (2013) define the process of impounding information into prices as "price discovery" and refer to "price efficiency" when talking about the informativeness of prices *(see Brogaard/Hendershott/Riordan 2013, p. 2)*. Efficient prices, so say financial economists, contribute to more informed financing and investment, resulting in better allocation of income and higher welfare *(see Foresight et al. 2012, p. 53)*. According to Grossman and Stiglitz (1980), fully efficient markets do not exist. They describe that companies will only gather information for the purpose of trading on it should the profits outweigh the additional costs related to the process. This, however, is impossible when prices already reflect all the information *(see Grossman/Stiglitz 1980, p. 393)*. Nevertheless, the literature on the matter suggests that HFT can indeed contribute to price discovery. This section of the paper aims to examine the influence of HFT on price discovery and the overall market quality.

Brogaard, Hendershott and Riordan (2013) use data which was made available by NASDAQ to explain the role of HFTs in the price discovery process *(see Brogaard/Hendershott/Riordan 2013, p. 1)*. This dataset includes several stocks that were traded in 2008 and 2009, showing if HFTs mainly placed liquidity demanding (marketable) or liquidity supplying (nonmarketable) orders. They explain the influence of HFTs on permanent and temporary changes in price movement and find that HFTs contribute to permanent price changes and reduce temporary pricing errors, which are also referred to as "transitory volatility" or "noise", under normal as well as stressful market conditions. Their liquidity demanding orders support this efficiency-increasing effect, whereas liquidity supplying orders counteract it *(see Brogaard/Hendershott/Riordan 2013, p. 2)*. Overall they find that HFT adds to price discovery and enhances price efficiency, indicating that the efficiency-increasing activity of HFTs prevails (see *Brogaard/Hendershott/Riordan 2013, p. 3)*.

Hendershott and Riordan (2009) define the role of AT in the price discovery process, based on an analysis of the 30 DAX-stocks on the Deutsche Boerse in 2008 *(see Hendershott/Riordan 2009, p. 1)*. They find that ATs add more to the discovery of the efficient price than human traders, and that their permanent price impact exceeds that of humans by approximately 20% *(see Hendershott/Riordan 2009, p. 3)*. Their results show that liquidity demanding trades of ATs result in prices that reflect 40% more information than the trades of humans *(see Hendershott/Riordan 2009, pp. 3-4)*. Furthermore, ATs contribute more to the discovery of the efficient price than human trading, as they have more efficient quotes *(see Hendershott/Riordan 2009, p. 4)*. It is found that the effect of the ATP that was approved by the German competition authority contributes to price efficiency *(see Hendershott/Riordan 2009, p. 23)*.

Brogaard (2010) examines the importance of HFT in the price discovery process by, firstly, illustrating the permanent price impact of HFT, secondly concentrating on the roles of HFTs and non-HFTs in the price formation process and, thirdly, analyzing the quotes placed by HFTs and non-HFTs *(see Brogaard 2010, pp. 31-32)*. He finds that HFTs contribute more to price discovery than human traders, whereas their impact on price discovery is higher than that of human traders in large stocks, equal to humans' in medium stocks and lower in small stocks *(see Brogaard 2010, p. 31)*. Furthermore, he suggests that HFTs are more often at the best bid and offer than human traders *(see Brogaard 2010, p. 40)*. This conforms to the findings of Hendershott and Riordan (2009), indicating that ATs contribute more to the discovery of the efficient price than humans *(see Hendershott/Riordan 2009, p. 4)*. Overall his results show that HFT increases market quality *(see Brogaard 2010, p. 40)*.

Zhang (2010) describes the influence of HFT on price discovery, based on a dataset from CRSP and the Thomson Reuters Institutional Holdings databases from 1985 to 2009 *(Zhang 2010, p. 2)*. He finds that HFT has a negative influence on price discovery, as prices tend to overreact to fundamental news in the presence of HFT. The changes in prices, caused by HFT, are mostly reversed shortly after their occurrence *(Zhang 2010, p. 34)*. Speculators may trade based on information unrelated to fundamental data *(Froot/Scharfstein/Stein 1992, p. 1461)*. Zhang relates this to HFT, implying that due to its activity in the market, efficient pricing seems impossible *(Zhang 2010, pp. 1-2)*. The overall results suggest that HFT hinders price discovery *(Zhang 2010, p. 34)*, indicating a negative influence on market quality.

The findings of the researchers quoted indicate that HFT contributes to long-term price changes rather than transitory price movements *(see Brogaard/Hendershott/Riordan 2013, p. 2)*, increase the degree of information reflected by prices *(see Hendershott/Riordan 2009, pp. 3-4)* and are frequently at the best bid and offer *(see*

Brogaard 2010, p. 40). These results reveal that HFT contributes to price discovery and thus improves overall market quality. Zhang (2010), however, refers to the research of Froot, Scharfenstein and Stein (1992), arguing that prices overreact to news when HFTs are present in the market, as they trade based on data that are not fundamental and thus they harm the discovery of the efficient price *(Zhang 2010, pp. 1-2)*. This is inconsistent with the results of Brogaard, Hendershott and Riordan (2013), implying that HFT reduces short-term pricing errors *(see Brogaard/Hendershott/Riordan 2013, p. 2)*. Their findings, indicating that liquidity demanding orders of HFTs contribute to long-term price changes and reduce transitory volatility, are favorable to market quality. However, Liquidity-supplying orders of HFTs tend to counteract this positive effect. *(see Brogaard/Hendershott/Riordan 2013, p. 2)*. Furthermore, according to Menkveld (2013), approximately 78% of HF-trades are passive (liquidity supplying) and only 22% are aggressive (liquidity demanding) *(see Menkveld 2013, p. 22)*.

3.4 The effect of HFT on volatility

Price volatility is an important measure of the stability/instability of financial markets *(see Foresight et al. 2012, p. 53)*. As HFT is often blamed for the occurrence of excess volatility and market instability *(see Brogaard 2011, p. 1)*, it is a frequently discussed topic in literature. There is research on the matter which indicates that HFT lowers price volatility *(see Brogaard 2011, p. 1; see Hasbrouck and Saar 2010, p. 3)* and such which describes that there is hardly any causal relationship between HFT and price volatility *(see Hendershott and Riordan 2009, p. 5)*. Other researchers indicate that HFT clearly increases volatility *(see Zhang 2010, p. 2; see Boehmer/Fong/Wu 2012, p. 3)*. In this chapter, the impact of HFT on price volatility and its influence on overall market quality is examined by comparing different research on the matter.

Brogaard (2011) uses data from the time of the economic and financial crisis of 2008 and 2009, a time of extraordinarily high volatility, in order to explain that HFT decreases intraday volatility on the stock market *(see Brogaard 2011, pp. 1-2)*. He measures the change in volatility when an exogenous shock occurs to HFT *(see Brogaard 2011, pp. 1-2)*. In particular, the short sale ban of September 2008 served as an example for the removal of several HFTs from the market *(see Brogaard 2011, p. 29)*. His sample allows a distinction of the activity of HFTs from that of non-HFTs and shows if HFTs, in case they participated in a trade, supplied or demanded liquidity. He established a direct connection between HFT and stock price volatility *(see Brogaard 2011, p. 2)* and found that the presence of HFTs in the financial markets of 2011 diminished volatility *(see Brogaard 2011, p. 29)*. This indicates a positive effect of HFT on the overall market quality.

Hasbrouck and Saar (2010) use real-time data from NASDAQ that provide detailed information about the trading activity on this exchange in two 10-minute sample periods, in October 2007 and June 2008, in order to measure the influence of HFT on stock volatility *(see Hasbrouck/Saar 2010, p. 2)*. They use "HighLow", the difference between the highest and the lowest midquote in an interval, as a measure of volatility *(see Hasbrouck/Saar 2010, p. 2)*. The results show that low-latency trading decreases volatility. Furthermore, they find that usually low-latency trading has similar effects on companies with small and such with large market capitalization. During times of market stress, however, it seems that low-latency activity reduces volatility of small stocks to a higher extent that that of large stocks *(see Hasbrouck/Saar 2010, p. 25)*. Their findings indicate a positive impact of HFT on the overall market quality.

Hendershott and Riordan (2009) inspect AT taking into account lagged volatility, the absolute value of the stock return over the 15 minutes prior to a transaction, among other things. The results show that in these 15 minutes, AT is unrelated to volatility *(see Hendershott/Riordan 2009, p. 13)*. They do not find any evidence that AT increases volatility beyond making prices more efficient *(see Hendershott/Riordan 2009, p. 23)*.

Zhang (2010) examines the influence HFT has on stock volatility *(see Zhang 2010, p. 1)*. He shows that it is not clear which exact effect HFT has on volatility, but he finds that the interaction between HFTs and fundamental investors may increase stock volatility for three reasons: (1) The high volume traded by HFTs is not always an indicator of liquidity – as illustrated in the Flash Crash in 2010. (2) HFTs often trade on short-term statistical correlations among stock returns, which can create price momentum and attract other momentum traders, causing higher volatility. (3) As already explained in chapter "2.4.2 Liquidity Detection", HFTs are able to detect and front-run large orders placed by institutional investors, pushing prices up or down and thus increasing volatility *(see Zhang 2010, p. 8)*. Furthermore, he explains that the positive correlation between HFT and stock volatility is stronger for stocks with higher market capitalization and high institutional holdings, especially during times of market stress *(see Zhang 2010, p. 22)*. Also, the fact that HFT causes overreactions of prices, which are corrected shortly after their occurrence, to fundamental data proves that HFT increases volatility *(see Zhang 2010, p. 35)* and thus has a negative effect on the overall market quality.

Boehmer, Fong and Wu (2012) use data from 39 major stock markets in order to examine the impact of AT on market quality, also referring to price volatility *(see Boehmer/Fong/Wu 2012, p. 27)*. The intra-day range between the highest and the lowest prices of a given day are used as the primary volatility-measure *(see Boehmer/Fong/Wu 2012, p. 15)*. The researchers find that AT consistently enlarges stock volatility across all markets *(see Boehmer/Fong/Wu 2012, p. 27)*, independent of a company's market capitalization and share price *(see Boehmer/Fong/Wu 2012, p. 25)*. It is explained that this volatility is not caused by more efficient prices, adjusting faster to new information *(see Boehmer/Fong/Wu 2012, p. 27)*, indicating that AT creates and increases excess volatility. This positive correlation between AT and volatility suggests a negative effect of AT on overall market quality.

Several of the researchers define a causal relationship between HFT and volatility *(see Brogaard 2011, p. 2)*, others, however describe that there is almost no connection between the two *(see Hendershott and Riordan 2009, p. 5)*. Of those who established a relationship between HFT and volatility, some provide evidence that HFT decreases volatility *(see Brogaard 2011, p. 29; see Hasbrouck/Saar 2010, p. 25)*, while others prove the exact opposite *(see Zhang 2010, p. 35; see Boehmer/Fong/Wu 2012, p. 27)*.

4 The regulation and supervision of HFT

In recent years HFT has become an important topic for market participants as well as regulators. The aim of the latter is to collect information in order to regulate HFT in an efficient way and react to developments that could cause a negative effect of HFT on market quality *(see Gomber et al. 2011, p. 39)*. This chapter illustrates the importance of the regulation of financial markets, for the purpose of reducing the negative effects of HFT on the quality of these markets, as well as measures taken to achieve this objective.

4.1 Manipulation and the importance of regulation and supervision of HFT

Institutional investors often describe high frequency trading as an instrument of market manipulation *(see Foresight et al. 2012, p. 87)*. In July 2013 an HFT was fined by the US CFTC, the UK Conduct Authority and CME Group, an exchanges operator, for manipulating futures markets over a three month period *(see Stafford/Massoudi/Meyer 2013)*. Biais and Woolley (2011) explain that HFT may engage in market manipulation in the form of "stuffing", "smoking" and "spoofing". "Stuffing" is the practice of placing large amounts of orders on the market, which makes it almost impossible for non-HFTs (slow traders) to get a true picture of the current trading situation as well as to access the market and execute trades. This way, HFTs (fast traders) can generate profits at the cost of non-HFTs. "Smoking" is defined as posting limit orders that are attractive for slow traders and then quickly changing the orders and hoping to benefit from the orders submitted by the attracted slow traders. "Spoofing" describes a strategy at which an HFT who, as an example, wants to buy, actually submits sell orders for a price above the highest ask price in order to make sure they are not executed. By placing these large sell orders, the HFT aims to scare other market participants and make them sell at relatively low prices. In the meantime the HFT will have placed buy-orders in order to take advantage of the peoples' panic and the resulting low prices *(see Biais/Woolley 2011, pp. 8-9)*. In her speech on September 22, 2010, SEC Chairman Mary Schapiro said that HFTs have tremendous capacity to affect the stability and integrity of the equity markets, and that HFTs had hardly any obligations to protect the stability of financial markets and to omit exacerbating price volatility *(see Schapiro 2010)*. It is not to be claimed that all HFTs engage in market manipulating activity, but the capability of HFTs to do so motivates regulatory bodies to constantly improve its regulation and supervision.

4.2 The Flash Crash

The necessity of proper regulation and supervision of HFT was very much realized after one event, the Flash Crash of May 06, 2010.

Due to negative economic news concerning the European debt crisis, the trading day started unusually turbulent. The negative price sentiment led to an increase in price volatility of several stocks. Yields of ten-year treasuries fell, and the resulting selling pressure led to a 2.5% drop of the DJIA. In the course of the flash crash, prices in futures and securities markets declined by up to 15% *(see U.S. Commodity Futures Trading Commission, the U.S. Security and Exchange Commission 2010, p. 1)*, whereas the DJIA lost approximately 9.2% at its worst, representing the largest intraday drop in the history of the index *(see Ortega Barrales 2012, p. 1233)*. Also the E-Mini S&P 500 as well as the S&P 500 SPDR ETF (SPY), two very frequently traded stock index instruments in electronic futures and equity markets, dropped dramatically. As volatility increased and market depth decreased, a large market participant initiated orders to sell E-Mini contracts, worth approximately USD 4.1 billion, to hedge an equity position. To execute these orders, this trader used an algorithm targeting neither price nor time but only trading volume, causing a net change in daily position, which was larger than that of any other trader since the beginning of 2010. HFTs bought these contracts from the large trader, but between 02:41 p.m. and 02:44 p.m. they started to sell them in order to reduce their long positions. HFTs traded almost 140.000 E-Mini contracts, amounting to 33% of the total trading volume. They caused a "hot potato effect" by buying and selling these contracts to each other very quickly. This quantity of trades led to a higher number of sell orders submitted by the large trader's algorithm. As a result, prices continued to decline until the CME Stop Logic Functionality was triggered at 02:45:28 p.m., stopping trading on the E-Mini for five seconds. Shortly after that, prices stabilized, and by 02:51 p.m. they were already increasing rapidly. Equity prices were still decreasing after the recovery of the E-Mini. Liquidity declined in several securities, leading to the execution of many trades at irrational prices. However, due to this low level of liquidity, traders had time to evaluate the data on which their trades were based. This resulted in the discovery of rational prices of the stocks by approximately 03:00 p.m. By the end of the trading day, futures as well as equity indices reported an intraday loss of approximately 3% *(see U.S. Commodity Futures Trading Commission, the U.S. Security and Exchange Commission 2010, pp. 1-6)*. Kirilenko et al. describe that HFTs were not responsible for the Flash Crash, but their reaction to the high selling pressure may have increased market volatility *(Kirilenko et al. 2011, p.1)*. Figure 3 illustrates the development of the DJIA-price on May 06, 2010. It shows a drop between 02:00 p.m. and 03:00 p.m., representing the Flash Crash.

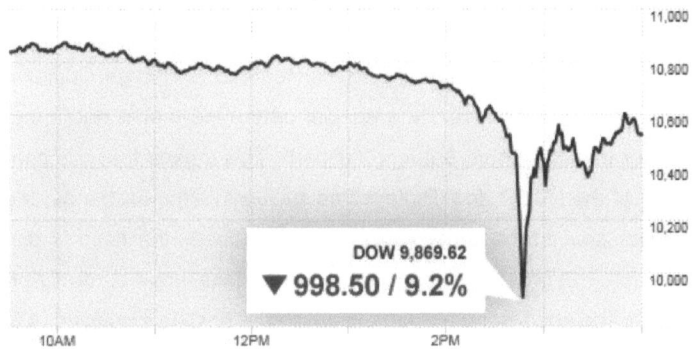

Figure 3: DJIA-Chart of May 06, 2010 *(see Rooney 2010)*

4.3 General regulatory measures

4.3.1 Unfiltered/Naked Sponsored Access

Most markets are directly accessible only by registered members, meaning that only they are allowed to trade. Such registered members, who serve as intermediaries for investors, are known as brokers. Brokers put their clients' investment plans into practice by submitting orders to trading venues. To save costs, other market access models, such as sponsored access, have been developed. Sponsored access allows non registered market participants to directly access the market, using a registered broker's member ID, without using the broker's infrastructure. As it helps to reduce latency, this system is especially attractive for HFTs. If exchanges do not provide brokers with the option of risk checks before the offer is executed, the broker is only informed about the trades made by its client in order to make it possible for him to check his own risk afterwards. With unfiltered/naked sponsored access, pre-trade risk checks are not possible *(see Gomber et al. 2011, p. 9)*. As a consequence, brokers cannot prevent the execution of erroneous orders *(see Gomber et al. 2011, p. 41)*. In 2010, the SEC proposed a rule, requiring brokers to implement a proper risk management and supervisory processes in order to be able to manage the risks resulting from this service *(see U.S. Securities and Exchange Commission 2010 b, p. 2)*. With the implementation of the rule in November 2010, the SEC effectively prohibited brokers and dealers with market access, from offering unfiltered market access to their customers.

4.3.2 Flash Orders

In general, U.S. trading venues are obliged to route orders to other exchanges if they cannot execute an order at the NBBO *(see U.S. Securities and Exchange Commission 2005, p. 36)*. A flash order, however, is a special order type that is not immediately routed to another trading venue, but first "flashed". This means that it is converted into a limit order at the NBBO and displayed as such within the exchange. If a trading partner executes against the order within the milliseconds the flash is displayed in the marketplace, the order will not be routed to the exchange currently offering the NBBO. Due to the short period of time in which the flash is displayed, it is almost impossible for non-HFTs to react *(see Gomber et al. 2011, p. 42)*. According to the SEC, flash orders may have numerous drawbacks. For instance, they discourage investors to display their trading interest by posting non-marketable limit orders which are important for price discovery, as they increase liquidity. Flash orders may deprive those traders, who quote at the NBBO, from getting their orders executed at that price *(see U.S. Securities and Exchange Commission 2009, pp. 17-18)*. As a result of the critique of flash orders, the SEC proposed a rule to ban flash orders in 2009 *(see U.S. Securities and Exchange Commission 2009, p. 1)*. In 2010 it was made possible again to comment on the proposed rule *(see U.S. Securities and Exchange Commission 2010 a, p. 1)*. NASDAQ and BATS, two major American stock exchanges, banned flash trading in August 2009, even before the prohibition of this technique was proposed by the SEC *(see Sukumar 2009)*.

4.4 The regulatory response to the Flash Crash

4.4.1 Circuit breakers

After the events of May 06, 2010, American trading venues developed circuit breaker rules, which were officially proposed to the SEC on May 18 and 19, 2010 *(see U.S. Securities and Exchange Commission 2010 c, p. 4)* and implemented as a pilot program by the Commission on June 10 of the same year *(see U.S. Securities and Exchange Commission 2010 c, pp. 5 and 13)*. These rules oblige the primary trading venues of S&P500-securities to halt trading in any of the individual securities for a five-minute period should its price move 10% or more within five minutes. Other exchanges have to be informed about the pause and are required to stop trading the respective security as well. After five minutes, the primary trading venue may restart trading it, which allows the other exchanges to reopen trading as well. If there is an imbalance on the primary trading venue after the five-minute pause, the trading halt can be extended. After ten minutes, however, the other exchanges may restart trading in the security, no matter if the primary trading venue reopened trading in the security *(see U.S. Securities and Exchange Commission 2010 c, pp. 4-6)*. In June 2011, the SEC approved a proposal to expand the circuit breaker rules to all NMS stocks *(see U.S. Securities and Exchange Commission 2011, pp. 1-2)*. Subrahmanyam (1994) explains that, under certain circumstances, such circuit breakers can increase volatility and reduce liquidity on the markets that are regulated with the help of this tool *(Subrahmanyam 1994, p. 250)*.

In April 2013, the first phase of a National Market system plan was implemented in order to replace the single-stock circuit breakers with a "limit up - limit down" mechanism. This mechanism shall prevent trades in NMS stocks from being executed if they are outside of certain price bands *(see U.S. Securities and Exchange Commission 2013, pp. 2-4)*.

4.4.2 Stub quotes and erroneous trades

Quotes that differ significantly from the current price of a security are called "stub quotes". Such quotes, that are not intended to ever be executed, are used by market makers to fulfill their quoting obligations. The high level of volatility during the Flash Crash, however, led to the execution of numerous stub quotes *(see Gomber et al. 2011, p. 46)*. In November 2010, the SEC approved rules, proposed by American trading venues as well as FINRA, requiring equity market makers to continuously quote within a certain range of the inside market *(see U.S. Securities and Exchange Commission 2010 d, pp. 1-2)* in order to prevent the existence of such quotes. Furthermore, the SEC developed standards for breaking clearly erroneous trades in case they occur. During the Flash Crash, there were no such specific rules. Exchanges chose to break trades that diverged 60% or more from the fair value. The rules adopted by the SEC after the Flash Crash require exchanges to break trades in stocks with associated circuit breakers, if their prices are either 10%, 5% or 3% away from the prices that trigger the circuit breakers. The percentage that applies to a specific stock depends on the stock price *(Chapman 2010, p. 1)*. According to SEC

Chairman Schapiro, the adoption of exact standards, describing when to break erroneous trades, makes it easier for exchanges to decide, which trades will be broken, and it also facilitates risk management for market participants *(see Lynch, 2010)*.

4.5 Other possible regulatory measures and their effect on volatility

4.5.1 Tobin tax

Tobin (1978) explains that excessive inter-currency mobility of private funds, resulting from the development of international financial markets that facilitate currency conversions, causes disturbances in those markets *(see Tobin 1978, pp. 2-3)*. To address this problem, he offered a proposal in his "Janeway Lectures" at Princeton, in 1972. He proposed the introduction of an international tax on all spot conversions between currencies, proportional to the size of the transaction. Tobin especially wanted to tax short-term currency conversions in order to decrease financial volatility by reducing speculation *(see Tobin 1978, p. 6)*. Also, Schulmeister (2009) describes that a minor tax on financial transactions (0.01%-0.1%) would specifically burden speculative short-term trading, whereas the investment in financial instruments, for the purpose of holding them, would hardly be taxed *(see Schulmeister 2009, p. 13)*. In 2013, Italy, as the first country to do so, introduced a financial transaction tax on HFT. Order changes and cancellations of HFTs are taxed at two basis points if they occur within less than half a second. This regulatory measure is thought to stabilize markets, reduce speculation and increase federal income *(see Stafford 2013)*. Buss et al. (2013) study the influence of a financial transactions tax, such as the Tobin Tax, on stock volatility. They find that stock volatility and consumption-growth volatility are increased by the Tobin Tax, whereas investment growth as well as output growth is reduced. The results indicate that the Tobin Tax does not reduce stock volatility and has an overall negative effect on market quality *(see Buss et al. 2013, pp. 19-20)*.

4.5.2 Short sale constraints

According to Beber and Pagano (2013), most regulators of stock markets reacted to the financial crisis of 2007-2009 by banning or constraining short sales *(see Beber, Pagano 2013, p. 343)*. In 2010, the SEC adopted a rule to prevent short selling from further decreasing stock prices which have already dropped by 10% or more, compared to the closing price of the previous day *(see U.S. Securities and Exchange Commission 2010 e, p. 1)*. Boehmer, Jones and Zhang (2009) examine the influence of the 2008 shorting ban on market quality. Their results indicate that market quality – in terms of intraday volatility and price impacts – was reduced severely *(Boehmer/Jones/Zhang 2009, p. 1)*. They also describe that the ban affected large-cap stocks more than small-cap stocks. The fact that HFTs tend to focus on trading liquid large-cap stocks is the reason why they were probably affected the most by the short sale ban *(Boehmer/Jones/Zhang 2009, p. 12)*. Beber and Pagano (2013) examine the influence of bans and constraints of short sales on market quality. They find that short sale constraints decrease market liquidity and have a negative influence on price discovery *(see Beber, Pagano 2013, p. 379)*. Buss et al. illustrate the effect of short sale constraints on price volatility. Their research provides evidence of an overall negative effect of short sale constraints on market stability, indicating that they increase, rather than reduce, stock volatility *(see Buss et al. 2013, pp. 19-20)*.

5 Conclusion

This paper compares different researchers' findings on the effects of HFT on market quality, focusing on liquidity, price discovery and volatility. A combination of the research results is necessary to provide a realistic description of the matter, as there is no single research that perfectly describes the overall effect of HFT on the quality of capital markets.

The results of the research stated in chapter "3.2 The effect of HFT on liquidity" indicate that HFTs narrow spreads, mainly provide liquidity and thus contribute to the discovery of the equilibrium price of a security. The fact that HFTs tend to supply liquidity when it is expensive and demand it when it is cheap may seem to put non-HFTs in a disadvantaged position, but it needs to be kept in mind that the reason why liquidity is expensive is, that there is not much of it in the market. This implies that HFTs provide other market participants with a chance to trade, even in situations when no one else is willing to provide that liquidity. HFTs often provide liquidity, which is necessary for price discovery. This influence on market quality is positive, indicating that HFT can be explained by the neoclassical theory of economics.

The research listed in chapter "3.3 The effect of HFT on price discovery" provides evidence that HFT increases the degree of information reflected in prices and contributes to long-term price changes rather than transitory price movements. Furthermore, HFTs often quote at the best bid and offer. Anyhow, it is also stated that HFT has characteristics that could cause an increase in the deviation between the real price and the equilibrium. Prices may overreact to news when HFTs are present on the market. This indicates that the influence of HFT on market quality is not solely positive, implying that HFT cannot be fully explained by the neoclassical theory of economics.

The results of the research invoked in chapter "3.4 The effect of HFT on volatility" indicate that the exact influence of HFT on volatility is unclear. According to some researchers, there is a causal relationship between HFT and volatility, others describe that the two are not connected. Of those who established a relation between the two, both, the ones implying that HFT decreases volatility as well as the ones describing that it increases volatility, provide evidence for their statement. It needs to be kept in mind that research on the basis of different data can provide different results, but as in the literature on the matter numerous different – and sometimes the most contrary – results are presented, it is not possible to clearly identify the real impact of HFT on stock volatility. However, it is identifiable that the impact of HFT on stock volatility, and thus its influence on the overall market quality, is not solely positive, indicating that HFT cannot be fully explained by the neoclassical theory of economics.

It is concluded that, due to its partly negative influence on price discovery and volatility, HFT cannot be fully explained by the neoclassical theory of economics. The system contravenes the first fundamental assumption of the theory, stating that agents – in this paper, this term also refers to trading computers – always act individually to achieve their goal, the maximization of profits or the personal well-being. Often, however, the actions of HFTs are triggered by other HFTs' activities, leading to chain reactions and excess volatility. Trading based on fundamental data does not allow for transactions at such a high frequency, implying that HFTs mainly base their trades on short-term estimations instead of fundamental data. As a result, HFTs do not fully support the reflection of the total relevant information in market prices. Their presence in financial markets may cause overreactions to market news and expose financial markets to the risk of excess volatility. Furthermore, the system of HFT contravenes the third rationality-assumption of the neoclassical theory of economics. It describes, that market participants act in the most rational way to achieve their individual goals, and does not leave room for the fallibility of human beings. As HFT-algorithms are programmed by people, who are vulnerable to external influences which can lead to irrational decision making and mistakes, the system cannot be fully explained by the neoclassical theory of economics.

Additionally, in chapter "4 The regulation and supervision of HFT", this work examines if the negative effects of HFT on market quality can be reduced to a sufficient extent in order for HFT to be fully explained by the neoclassical theory of economics. For that purpose, several regulatory measures are investigated.

By prohibiting unfiltered/naked sponsored access, the SEC made it impossible for traders, who are not registered members, to directly access markets. As a consequence, only registered members can engage in HFT. This way, it can be ensured that regulators and exchanges have the opportunity to find out who is responsible for specific trading activities *(Patterson 2010)*. The prohibition of naked access improves transparency in financial markets and facilitates governmental supervision. However, it does not limit the capabilities of HFTs, and thus it has no direct influence on the effect of HFT on liquidity, price discovery and volatility.

Following the SEC, a ban of flash orders would motivate investors to place more non-marketable limit orders and thus add liquidity and contribute to price discovery. However, the negative impact of HFT on price discovery and volatility, reported by Zhang (2010), is not reduced by this regulatory measure. He describes that prices overreact to news when HFTs are present on the market, as they trade based on information that is not fundamental. (See chapter "3.3 The effect of HFT on price discovery"). According to SEC-Chairman Schapiro, circuit breakers shall reduce volatility. From the Flash Crash we know that a short trading halt can cause a stabilization of prices. However, Subrahmanyam (1994) describes that, under certain circumstances, this regulatory instrument can increase volatility and reduce liquidity. Furthermore, circuit breakers are only triggered if price movements are very high already. The "Limit Up-Limit Down Plan" implemented in 2013 is found to have a more positive effect on market quality, as it prevents quotes at irrational prices from being executed in the first place.

Also, a ban on stub quotes as well as the implementation of clear rules, defining when to break erroneous trades, is found to have a volatility-reducing and thus positive effect on the overall market quality.

The implementation of the Tobin Tax may have positive influence on federal income. The findings concerning its effect on market volatility, however, are mixed. Buss et al. (2013) provide evidence that this effect is clearly negative.

Short sale constraints are found to have a liquidity-decreasing effect and hinder price discovery. Furthermore, they tend to increase price volatility.

It is concluded that, by employing strict regulation of financial markets, the negative effects of HFT on market quality cannot be reduced to a sufficient extent in order for the system to be fully explained by the neoclassical theory of economics. Regulators continuously strive to organize financial markets as secure and transparent as possible, but due to the high speed, the large number of trades, the complexity of the infrastructure used as well as the difficulties in supervising the system, HFT is related to uncertainties and dangers. Some of the regulatory measures implemented do improve market quality, but they do not suffice to eliminate HFTs' capabilities of influencing financial markets in a negative way.

References

1. Literature

Books

Lee, R. (1998): *What is an exchange?, The Automation, Management and Regulation of Financial Markets*, Oxford: Oxford University Press.

Polanyi, K. (1944): *The Great Transformation*, Beacon Press, Boston, USA.

Dissertations

Gomolka, J. (2011): *Algorithmic Trading – Analyse von computergesteuerten Prozessen im Wertpapierhandel unter Verwendung der Multifaktorenregression*, Dissertation, Universität Potsdam.

Journal Articles

Beber, A., Pagano, M. (2013): *Short-Selling Bans Around the World: Evidence from the 2007-09 Crisis*, The Journal of Finance, Vol. 68, Issue 1, pp. 343-381.

Brennan, G., Moehler, M. (2010): *Neoclassical Economics*, Encyclopedia of Political Theory, ed. Mark Bevir (SAGE Publications), Vol. 2, pp. 946-951.

Bresser-Pereira, L.C. (2012): *For a heterodox mainstream economics: an academic manifesto*, Journal of Post Keynesian Economics, Vol. 35, Issue 1, pp. 3-20.

Dequech, D. (2007): *Neoclassical, mainstream, orthodox and heterodox economics*, Journal of Post Keynesian Economics, Vol. 30, Issue 2, pp. 279-302.

Fama, E.F. (1970): *Efficient Capital Markets: A Review of Theory and Empirical Work*, The Journal of Finance, Vol. 25, Issue 2, pp. 383-417.

Froot, K.A., Scharfstein, D.S., Stein J.C. (1992): *Herd on the Street: Informational Inefficiencies in a Market with Short-Term Speculation*, The Journal of Finance, Vol. 47, Issue 4, pp. 1461-1484.

Grossman, S.J., Stiglitz, J.E. (1980): *On the Impossibility of Informationally Efficient Markets*, The American Economic Review, Vol. 70, Issue 3, pp. 393-408.

Hendershott, T., Jones, C.M., Menkveld, A.J. (2011): *Does Algorithmic Trading Improve Liquidity?*, Journal of Finance, Vol. 66, Issue 1, pp. 1-33.

Jain, P.K. (2005): *Financial Market Design and the Equity Premium: Electronic vs. Floor Trading,* Journal of Finance, Vol. 60, Issue 6, pp. 2955-2985.

Mori, M., Ziobrowski, A.J. (2011): *Performance of Pairs Trading Strategy in the U.S. REIT Market*, Real Estate Economics, Vol. 39, Issue 3, pp. 409-428.

Subrahmanyam, A. (1994): *Circuit Breakers and Market Volatility: A Theoretical Perspective*, Journal of Finance, Vol. 49, Issue 1, pp. 237-254.

Zadorozhny, V., Raschid, L., Gal, A. (2008): *Scalable Catalog Infrastructure for Managing Access Costs and Source Selection in Wide Area Networks*, International Journal of Cooperative Information Systems, Vol. 17, Issue 1, pp. 77-109.

Research Reports

Authority for the Financial Markets (AFM) (2010): *The application of advanced trading technology in the European marketplace*, Report, Amsterdam.

Foresight et al. (2012): *The Future of Computer Trading in Financial Markets*, Final Project Report, The Government Office for Science, London.

U.S. Commodity Futures Trading Commission, the U.S. Security and Exchange Commission (2010): *Findings regarding the market events of May 6, 2010*, Report, Washington.

Working Papers

Angel, J., Harris, L., Spatt, C. S. (2010*): Equity Trading in the 21st Century,* Marshall Research Paper Series, Working Paper FBE 09-10, University of Southern California.

Biais, B., Woolley, P. (2011): *High Frequency* Trading, Working Paper, Toulouse School of Economics and London School of Economics.

Boehmer, E., Fong, K., Wu, J. (2012): *International Evidence on Algorithmic Trading*, SSRN Working Paper.

Boehmer, E., Jones, C.M., Zhang, X. (2009): *Shackling Short Sellers: The 2008 Shorting Ban*, Working Paper, Columbia Business School.

Brogaard, J. A. (2010): *High Frequency Trading and its impact on market quality*, Working Paper, Northwestern University, Kellog School of Management.

Brogaard, J. A. (2011): *High Frequency Trading and Volatility,* Working Paper, Northwestern University, Kellogg School of Management.

Brogaard, J., Hendershott, T., Riordan, R. (2013): *High Frequency Trading and Price Discovery,* SSRN Working Paper.

Buss, A., Dumas, B., Uppal, R., Vilkov, G. (2013): *Comparing Different Regulatory Measures to Control Stock Market Volatility: A General Equilibrium Analysis,* Working Paper, INSEAD Business School, France.

Chami Batista, J., Borges da Silveira, G. (2008): *Trade costs and Deviations from the Law of One Price,* Working Paper, Federal University of Rio de Janeiro, Institute of Economics.

Gomber, P., Arndt, B., Lutat, M., Uhle, T. (2011): *High-Frequency Trading,* SSRN Working Paper.

Gomber, P., Lutat, M. (2007): *Pricing Engineering for Electronic Financial Markets,* SSRN Working Paper.

Hasbrouck, J., Saar, G. (2010): *Low-Latency Trading,* Stern School of Business Working Paper.

Hendershott, T., Riordan, R. (2009): *Algorithmic Trading and Information,* NET Institute Working Paper No.09-08.

Jones, C.M. (2013): *What Do We Know About High-Frequency Trading?,* Columbia Business School Research Paper No. 13-11.

Kirilenko, A.A., Kyle, A.S., Samadi, M., Tuzun, T. (2011): *The Flash Crash: The Impact of High Frequency Trading on an Electronic Market,* SSRN Working Paper.

Menkveld, A.J. (2013): *High Frequency Trading and the New-Market makers,* SSRN Working Paper.

Ortega Barrales, E. (2012): *Lessons from the Flash Crash for the Regulation of High-Frequency Traders,* Working Paper, Fordham Journal of Corporate & Financial Law.

Schulmeister, S. (2009): *Eine generelle Finanztransaktionssteuer – Konzept, Begründung, Auswirkungen,* WIFO Working Paper No.352.

Tobin, J. (1978): *A Proposal for International Monetary Reform,* Cowles Foundation discussion paper No. 506.

Zhang, F. (2010): *High-Frequency Trading, Stock Volatility and Price Discovery,* SSRN working paper.

2. Juridical Sources

U.S. Securities and Exchange Commission (2005): *Final Rules and amendments to joint industry plans: Regulation NMS*, 17 CFR Parts 200, 201, 230, 240, 242, 249, and 270, Release No. 34-51808, File No. S7-10-04, http://www.sec.gov/rules/final/34-51808.pdf, accessed September 2013.

U.S. Securities and Exchange Commission (2009): *Elimination of Flash Order Exception from Rule 602 of Regulation NMS*, Proposed rule, 17 CFR Part 242, Release No. 34-60684, File No. S7-21-09, http://www.sec.gov/rules/proposed/2010/34-62445.pdf, accessed September 2013.

U.S. Securities and Exchange Commission (2010) a: *Elimination of Flash Order Exception from Rule 602 of Regulation NMS*, Proposed rule, reopening of comment period, 17 CFR Part 242, Release No. 34-62445, File No. S7-21-09, http://www.sec.gov/rules/proposed/2010/34-62445.pdf, accessed September 2013.

U.S. Securities and Exchange Commission (2010) b: Risk Management Controls for Brokers or Dealers with Market Access, 17 CFR PART 240, Release No. 34-61379, File No. S7-03-10, http://www.sec.gov/rules/proposed/2010/34-61379.pdf, accessed September 2013.

U.S. Securities and Exchange Commission (2010) c: *Order Granting Accelerated Approval to Proposed Rule Changes Relating to Trading Pauses Due to Extraordinary Market Volatility*, Release No. 34-62252, File Nos. SR-BATS-2010-014; SR-EDGA-2010-01; SR-EDGX-2010-01; SR-BX-2010-037; SR-ISE-2010-48; SR-NYSE-2010-39; SR-NYSEAmex-2010-46; SR-NYSEArca-2010-41; SR-NASDAQ-2010-061; SR-CHX-2010-10; SR-NSX-2010-05; SR-CBOE-2010-047, http://www.sec.gov/rules/sro/bats/2010/34-62252.pdf, accessed September 2013.

U.S. Securities and Exchange Commission (2010) d: *Order Granting Accelerated Approval to Proposed Rule Changes, as Modified by Amendment No. 1, to Enhance the Quotation Standards for Market Makers*, Release No. 34-63255, File Nos. SR-BATS-2010-025; SR-BX-2010-66; SR-CBOE-2010-087; SR-CHX-2010-22; SR-FINRA-2010-049; SR-NASDAQ-2010-115; SR-NSX-2010-12; SR-NYSE-2010-69; SR-NYSEAmex-2010-96; SR-NYSEArca-2010-83, http://www.sec.gov/rules/sro/bats/2010/34-63255.pdf, accessed September 2013.

U.S. Securities and Exchange Commission (2010) e: *Amendments to Regulation SHO*, Final rule, 17 CFR PART 242, Release No. 34-61595; File No. S7-08-09, http://www.sec.gov/rules/final/2010/34-61595.pdf, accessed September 2013.

U.S. Securities and Exchange Commission (2011): *Order Approving Proposed Rule Changes Relating to Expanding the Pilot Rule for Trading Pauses Due to Extraordinary Market Volatility to all NMS stocks*, Release No. 34-64735, File Nos. SR-BATS-2011-016; SR-BYX-2011-011; SR-BX-2011-025; SR-CBOE-2011-049; SR-CHX-2011-09; SR-EDGA-2011-15; SR-EDGX-2011-14; SR-FINRA-2011-023; SR-ISE-2011-028; SR-NASDAQ-2011-067; SR-NYSE-2011-21; SR-NYSEAmex-2011-32; SR-NYSEArca-2011-26; SR-NSX-2011-06; SR-Phlx-2011-64,

http://www.sec.gov/rules/sro/bats/2011/34-64735.pdf, accessed September 2013.

U.S. Securities and Exchange Commission (2013): *Order Approving, on an Accelerated Basis, Prposed Rule Change Relating to Limit Up Limit Down Functionality*, Release No. 34-69354; File No. SR-MIAX-2013-15,

http://www.sec.gov/rules/sro/miax/2013/34-69354.pdf, accessed September 2013.

3. Other References

Online References

Foroohar, K. (2010): *Trading Pennies Into $7 Billion Drives High-Frequency's Cowboys*, Bloomberg Markets Magazine, http://www.bloomberg.com/news/2010-10-06/trading-pennies-into-7-billion-profit-drives-high-frequency-s-new-cowboys.html, accessed July 2013.

Lynch, S.N. (2010): *SEC Proposes Rules for Erroneous Trades*, The Wall Street Journal, http://online.wsj.com/article/SB10001424052748704289504575313010186620470.html#articleTabs%3Darticle, accessed August 2013.

Patterson, S. (2010): *SEC Proposes Banning "Naked Access"*, Wall Street Journal, http://online.wsj.com/article/SB10001424052748704362004575000962550983250.html#, accessed September 2013.

Rooney, B. (2010): *Trading program sparked May "flash crash"*, CNN Money, http://money.cnn.com/2010/10/01/markets/SEC_CFTC_flash_crash/index.htm, accessed September 2013.

Schapiro, M.L. (2010): *Speech by SEC Chairman: Remarks Before the Security Traders Association*, http://www.sec.gov/news/speech/2010/spch092210mls.htm, accessed September 2013.

Stafford, P. (2013): *Italy introduces tax on high-speed trade and equity derivatives*, Financial Times, http://www.ft.com/intl/cms/s/0/378dcace-117e-11e3-8321-00144feabdc0.html#axzz2e94cZCkJ, accessed September 2013.

Stafford, P., Massoudi A., Meyer, G. (2013): *High-frequency trader fined in transatlantic clampdown*, Financial Times, http://www.ft.com/intl/cms/s/0/c0349552-f2d8-11e2-a203-00144feabdc0.html#axzz2dNRGC7b0, accessed August 2013.

Sukumar, N. (2009): *Nasdaq, Bats to Stop Allowing Flash Orders for Stocks (Update 5)*, Bloomberg, http://www.bloomberg.com/apps/news?pid=newsarchive&sid=atYLu1C6WDzo, accessed September 2013.

Other articles

Chapman, P. (2010): *Traders Digest The "Clearly Erroneous"*, in: Traders Magazine, Vol. 23, Issue 314, pp. 20-22.

Gomber, P. (2011): *Zwischen Nutzeffekten und Risiken*, in: Börsen-Zeitung Nr. 168, S. 19.

Kumar, P., Goldstein, M., Graves, F., Borucki, L. (2011): *Trading at the Speed of Light: The Impact of High-Frequency Trading on Market Performance, Regulatory Oversight, and Securities Litigation*, in: Finance – Current Topics in Corporate Finance and Litigation (The Brattle Group), Issue 02/2011, pp. 1-12.

Reynolds, K. (2011): *Gaming 101: Liquidity Detection*, in: Traders Magazine, Vol. 24, Issue 323, p. 24-24.

Sietmann, R. (2011): *Wettrüsten – Wertpapierhändler investieren in schnelle Netze*, in: C't Magazin für Computertechnik, Jg. 2011, Heft 12, S. 150-155.

Watson, T. (2011): *Rise of the Machines*, in: Canadian Business, Vol. 84, Issue 9, pp. 56-59.

Table of figures

Origin	Date of publication	US	Europe	Australia
TABB Group	Sep-09	61%		
Celent	Dec-09	42% of US trade volume	Rapidly growing	
Rosenblatt Securities	Sep-09	66%	~35% and growing fast	
Broogard	Nov-10	68% of Nasdaq trade volume		
Jarnecic and Snape	Jun-10		20% and 32% of LSE total trades and 19% and 28% of total volume	
Tradeworx	Apr-10	40%		
ASX	Feb-10			10% of ASX trade volume
Swinburne	Nov-10	70%	40%	
TABB Group	Jan-11		35% of overall UK market and 77% of turnover in continuous markets	

Figure 1: HFT Market shares from industry and academic studies *(Gomber et al. 2011, p. 73)*.

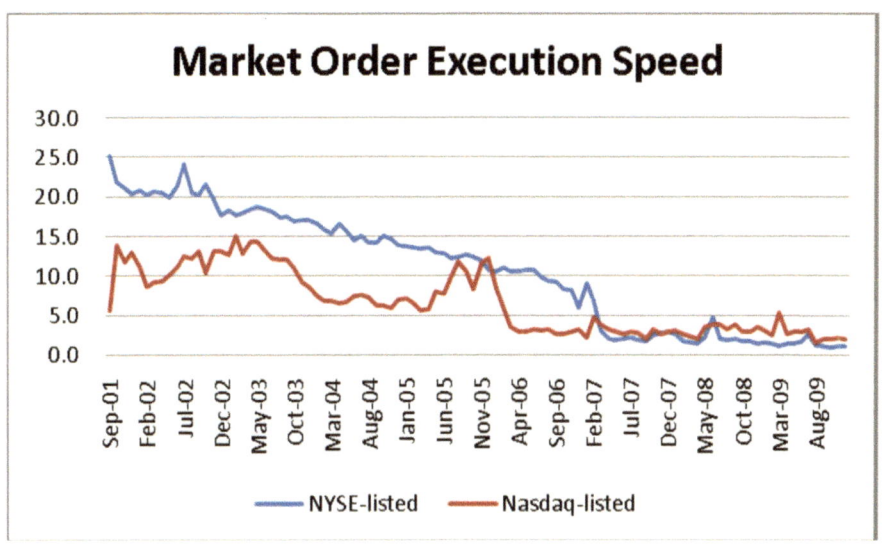

Figure 2: Market Order Execution Speed. Rule 605 data from Thomson for all eligible market orders (100-9999 shares) *(Angel/Harris/Spatt 2010, p. 38)*.

Figure 3: DJIA-Chart of May 06, 2010 *(Rooney 2010)*.